SUMMARY OF

FACT
FUL
NESS:

TEN REASONS WE'RE WRONG ABOUT THE WORLD--AND WHY THINGS ARE BETTER THAN YOU THINK

Proudly Brought To You By

BOOK ADDICT

WITH KEY POINTS
&
KEY TAKE AWAY

Disclaimer

This book is a summary and meant to be a great companionship to the original book or to simply help you get the gist of the original book. If you're looking for the original book, kindly go to Amazon website, and search for Factfulness by Hans Rosling.

Table of Contents

EXECUTIVE SUMMARY

Ever wondered why the world appears gloomy most of the time?

No, it's not just because the media is replete with bad news.

What if you were told that your biological disposition is largely responsible for why you think the world is worse off than it really is? What if you realize how misguided you have been in your assessment of the world?

This is the premise of *"Factfulness: Ten reasons we're wrong about the world – And why things are better than you think"*

In this book, Hans Rosling- in conjunction with Ola Rosling and Anna Rosling Rönnlund- discusses 10 instincts that have so far succeeded in twisting our view of the world. He also identifies practical steps through which we can overcome the hold of such inclinations. He provides facts and figures to support his assertion that contrary to popular opinion, the world is getting better and not worse.

Details in this book reveal inherent weaknesses that many of us remain unconscious of, and sadly, the resultant distorted worldview continues to affect every human industry; our actions and day-to-day living.

If you're ready to be shocked, if you're ready to be confronted with tough facts about how your mind has been working against you, and most importantly, if you're ready to see the world in a whole new light, then you should read this.

CHAPTER ONE: THE GAP INSTINCT

Key Takeaways:

- *Humans carry a primal instinct to be dramatic, pitch one extreme against another, and divide things into two opposing categories.*
- *Most of what we think we know about the world today are just emotions.*
- *Largely, we still carry on a worldview that dates as far back as 1965.*
- *The key to changing our worldview is to embrace facts.*
- *We must avoid seeing issues in averages and extremes.*

An insightful class in 1995 turned out to be the kick-start for my life journey on the path of contesting global delusions. After handing out data sheets to my students and asking them the child mortality rates in certain countries perceived as developing and under-developed, I realized they were less hesitant to reel out the current rates than they were to mention the rates from 35 years back. Their prevalent views about the world in which they lived did not align with the obvious fact that these countries had actually made progress in child mortality at a faster rate than some countries popularly perceived as developed. I realized they might not have believed me had they not been holding on to fact documents from UNICEF.

This realization was much more significant because an improvement in child mortality rates signaled an improvement in general quality of life as well. My students were not just coming to realize that the number of children who died below age 5 in these countries was way lower than it was 35 years ago. They were also coming to terms with the fact that these countries were generally better than they were 35 years ago. This was obviously not in line with what they had believed all along.

That day, my eyes were opened to an inherent dramatic predisposition- the first out of ten- responsible for our dominant perceptions (or more accurately, misperceptions) and beliefs about the world today. It is the tendency for us humans to place things into opposite categories and presume the existence of a huge gap between both. Thus, we have hurriedly placed every country and person in either of two boxes- rich or poor. We imagine an insane amount of unfairness exists to make the situation what it is, and this pretty much sets the tone for how we view everything in our world. Even after I explained how peculiar climatic conditions played a role in child mortality, my students were fixated on the belief that there was no way folks in rural areas and rainforests could live like they did because both were just in different categories. They emphasized how those folks had more children because they were not western, yet they found it difficult to firmly define these categories. When one of them attempted to define this categorization, I was elated. Not because she got it right but because she was so sure of her deduction- which was wrong- and I had the opportunity of putting up her belief against existing statistics.

Since that time, I have invested myself into the correction of these global fallacies. My son and daughter-in-law were impressed and inspired by the work I was doing, and in a bid to further this cause, they came up with the bubble chart- an ingenious way of presenting large data to squash the fallacy that the world is somehow partitioned into two opposites.

As it turns out, my students were not the only ones with this ideology- west/rest; rich/poor; developing/developed, etc. The whole world was along for the ride. We hear it in the media all the time. Political figures, economic experts, advocates and a bunch of other folks subscribe to these classifications that firmly keeps countries of the world segregated. People use these classifications so easily that hardly do they stop to think about what imagery it produces in their heads, and how those images measure up to the real situation.

Take, for instance, in 1965, a chart showing how many children women had on average across the globe would neatly place the world in two boxes- developing and developed. The developing were those countries with higher numbers of babies per women and higher child mortality rates while countries where women generally had fewer children and recorded fewer child deaths were classified as developed. Today, the story is not the same. Going by that classification, eighty-five percent of the world is developed because they record fewer babies per woman and fewer child deaths. Sadly, however, the prevailing worldview- especially in the west- is still stuck in 1965, with most countries confined to the 'developing' box.

This position gives us a very lopsided perspective of our world and sadly, informs our actions. It would interest you to also know that this reality is not restricted to child mortality only. In virtually every facet of human life, the world is improving. Most of the countries are making advancements, and so there is virtually none left in that developing box. The earlier we all understand and accept that there's no huge chasm dividing the world into west and non-west, rich and poor, etc., the better for us.

To say I was shocked by my students' responses is an understatement. I could not wrap my head around how vibrant, globally conscious minds such as theirs could still be holding on to a worldview that reflects the reality of years past. I could not understand how they easily subscribed to the notion of us versus them- the haves who had everything going for them and the have-nots who could never attain the standard of living enjoyed by the former. That class in 1995 lit a fire inside of me. With the use of statistical figures, I had helped to crumble the delusional opinions and beliefs which my students had held for so long. But they were only a fraction of the world's population that was held in the same grip of falsehood. Most of what we think we know are actually sentiments and not reality.

By 2015, this incorrect worldview was sadly, still very much held by the world. We still believed there existed a clear line dividing the world into developing and developed. On a television interview in Denmark, a journalist- who one would believe should be informed- intensely questioned my assertion that no such gap exists anymore. Even after I gave him figures- told him that 75% of the world's population now live comfortable middle-income lives- he still expressed doubt in the source of my claims. I told him there was nothing hidden about my sources; United Nations figures and the World Bank figures were accessible to anybody who cared to look. The truth is right where we can reach it, so why do we stay stuck on illusions?

I have been on this path long enough not to be shocked at the misconceptions people carry. In fact, the bulk of folks I come across with are holding on to these falsehoods as the current state of the world. One of our common tests provides evidence of this. When people were asked the primary school completion rate for girls in low-income countries, they went for the option with the lowest figure. In other words, many people automatically assume that the number of girls who finish primary education in so-called low-income countries is very low. As it turns out, the correct answer is the highest figure contained in those options. Sadly, this trend cuts across every question covering various issues like life expectancy, vaccination, water. Etc. Most people always go for the worst options even when those options indicate a quality of life only obtainable in times of utter disaster in extremely dreadful places.

It has been established that folks generally think the worst of life in low-income nations, but just how many people do they imagine to be living in these appalling conditions? The popular response for this was fifty percent or more but again, this assumed figure could not have been farther from the truth. The fact is, only nine percent- a tiny sum indeed- of the world's population can be found in these low-income countries, and as we have seen already, they are not as hopeless as the majority of the world make them out to be. It gets tricky here though: since only nine percent live in these so-called poor countries, where is the majority of the world then? In the 'rich' countries?

Our misguided belief that the world is divided into two opposite sides with a yawning gap in-between has kept us blind to the fact that there is a middle, not a gap. We have low-income countries and high-income countries, but, borrowing a leaf from this classification, there is also a middle, and this is where the majority- 75%- of the world's population reside. Accepting this fact holds huge significance for us all, especially globally-inclined businesses that fail to penetrate potential markets because they carry the notion that those folks are the 'have-nots'.

I do not particularly care for the term "developing countries" because it has only done more harm than good. Enough of carting the world into two boxes labeled "rich" and "poor", because it's just not that simple. We are so obsessed with labels that we do not see the dangers of oversimplifying human beings- untapped business potential and mismanaged relief allocation. Instead of splitting the world into two broad categories that do not reflect reality, we can use a distribution that informed by levels of income.

In this case, there will be four levels. Currently, the bulk of our world can be found in levels 2 and 3, the two mid-levels. It means most of the world has access to basic necessities of life. Thinking in terms of these four income levels, instead of the previous unrepresentative two, will help you view the world better and realistically. It will not only set the tone for absorbing every other thing you will read in this book, but will also empower you to make better-informed life decisions. The levels can be likened to the typical video game- everyone wants to move from level one. Unlike video games, however, level one is the toughest.

Level one makes up for about 1 billion of today's human population. Here, you'll find people living on $1 per day. They lack basic necessities and cannot afford typically simple things like good clothing, housing, education, transportation, healthcare, nourishing food, potable water, and healthy cooking methods.

Level two makes up for about 3 billion of today's human population. Here, you'll find people living on $4 per day. They can afford to buy food and eat some protein. There is no extravagance here but they can at least access basic needs like clothing, electricity, transportation, healthy cooking methods, and potable water. They still cannot afford optimum healthcare on their income and their electricity is epileptic at best.

Level three makes up for about 2 billion of today's human population. Here, you'll find people living on

$16 per day. They have access to running water, stable electricity, quality healthcare, personal means of transportation, high level of education, and jobs that pay better. They can even afford to have inexpensive fun such as a day at the beach.

Level four makes up for about 1 billion of today's human population. Here, you'll find people living on $64 per day. They have a high level of education and well-paying jobs. They can afford to buy a lot of things, take flights to go on vacations, get a car, and install water heaters in their homes. The problem with this level is that, because they have a lot, they tend to find it difficult to grasp the reality of folks living on other levels.

In reality, progressing from level one to four can take a family many generations. This income level system provides a clearer picture of the world's reality, discarding the erroneous belief that there are two broad kinds of people. More than that, it also presents the hope of moving up the ladder unlike the 'Us versus Them' fixed positions portrayed by the current worldview. The human race itself has come a long way. Starting out from level one, today its majority is spread out across levels 2 and 3. And no, this is not a recent development. It has been so for many years now.

You'll be wrong to underestimate the hold of our predisposition to have a gap in existence. No surprise here: even the World Bank hesitated for years before finally retiring the 'developed-developing' classification and a couple of other worldwide organizations, like the United Nations, are still yet to effect the adjustment.

You would think accepting facts should be easy, but against our primal human instinct, it doesn't stand a chance. We have a dramatic predisposition to pitch one extreme against another, leaving a gaping hole in between. We also find it easier to just split things up into two categories; it reduces the processing load of our brains. It is this primal instinct that the media capitalizes on, showcasing stories of extreme poverty or extreme wealth, pitching one side against the opposite side, building movie plots around the 'good versus evil' narrative. Why? Because of sensationalism appeal to our basic instincts. This predisposition to assume the existence of a gap is what leads us to assume there's conflict when there is none.

To view the world realistically and avoid being swept away by sensational generalizations, you must know how to curb this instinct. One way to do this is to be wary of average figures. It's too easy to look at an average and deduce a gap between two human groups or entities. Considering the groups individually provides a more accurate picture, and more often than not, you come to realize that there really is no gap. This is not disputing the fact that there are realities in which gaps exist. Take the South-African apartheid for example. Apartheid, however, was not a typical situation.

I mentioned earlier that we have a primal disposition towards extremes. Sadly, they only serve to distort our worldview by promoting our gap disposition. We are so focused on the extremes that we fail to consider the middles where the bulk of human population belong. It is no wonder our perspectives on the world are mostly skewed.

Living on level four, it can be challenging to cultivate a worldview based on facts. For one, you're unable to relate with the real situation of folks living on other levels. To compound matters, your primary source of information about how people on other levels live is the media, which is filled with spectacular events and almost nothing of every day, real life. Your perspective as a level four member is from the top, and from that exalted position, it's normal and seemingly reasonable to categorize the people down there as 'have-nots' without giving thought to their varying differences. Furthermore, this also strengthens the narrow 'developed-developing' classification.

From experience, I have gathered that folks on levels one to three are usually conscious of the differences. They know how much can change in their lives if only they moved up one more level. In your quest to adopt a fact-based worldview, you must first do away with the 2-category worldview that promotes division and conflict. Your next step will be to learn this new classification based on income levels. Then, you'll truly be on your way because, as you will see, this classification will be used to explain virtually everything that concerns our world. Thinking in terms of these levels will give you a clearer picture of the world we live in and help you understand it better. As crucial as data is to this journey, it would be difficult to overthrow the faulty worldview without an equally-simple, more suitable alternative. The four-level classification has that part covered.

CHAPTER TWO: THE NEGATIVITY INSTINCT

Key Takeaways:

- *We are naturally inclined to pay attention to the negative than the positive.*
- *This tendency is fueled by grim media reports and activists with skewed statistics.*
- *We must come to accept that unpleasant issues still exist and it doesn't negate the fact that the world is progressing.*
- *A focus on the negatives robs us of hope and strength to create an even better world.*

A very long time ago, when I was age four, I was at my grandparents' house when my curiosity got the better of me. That day, I ended up face-down in a sewage ditch that was anything but nice. Had it not been for my grandmother's timely rescue, I would have died. My mother was very ill at the time and my father worked long hours that kept him away from home a lot. During the weekend when we went visiting my mother at the hospital, mom was never allowed to come close to us nor us to her. According to my father, we could get infected by being too close to her. She would put on a smile for me and always tried to speak to me from the third floor where she was standing. But I only heard the wind.

Our inclination to notice negatives more than we do the positives is responsible for the second fallacy- the belief that the world is getting worse every day. I know I have heard that more times than I can count, and I even agree that there are some unpleasant things going on in the world today. Terrorism, war, water pollution, and greenhouse emissions are only some of the problems facing us today.

The saying goes that no man is an island, and so it is for every country. If we're going to achieve our collective goals as a world, then we will all have to pool resources to work. Let's not forget that we must all share a perception of the world that derives from facts. Sadly, the majority of us either do not know or what we know is a misconception. For instance, when people were asked whether they thought the world is getting better, or worse, or remains the same, majority chose the second option. What's interesting is that the respondents who answered this question are from across 30 countries. Is it a surprise then that many people IN today's world are battling chronic stress?

The bad news is everywhere; easily accessible. Not so with good news though. Countless advancements are being made all over the world even as we speak but it appears they do not carry enough weight or are not as dramatic as the bad news. You'll be surprised to learn how very little we know about progress being made around the world.

When I deliver lectures and share my data, I get a lot of surprised and inspired faces who had no idea just how better the world really is. Now, there usually is nothing special about the facts I dish out. My audience are just so uplifted because they typically have a negative mindset and they've had it for so long that any data that contradicts their negative perceptions are welcomed enthusiastically.

In one of our numerous online polls, we asked people what they thought: in the past 20 years, had the number of people living in abject poverty doubled, remained the same, or halved? As usual, most people got the answer wrong. Their minds could not fathom that the amount was halved. Back in 1800, a huge percentage- 85%- of the human population lived in abject poverty. As unbelievable as it may sound, countries like Sweden and the United Kingdom experienced high levels of starvation, sometimes resulting in deaths.

From 1800 however, that rate has been plummeting, with countries like China having half a billion fewer people in abject poverty than they did 20 years ago. Ordinarily, we should be elated, but our Television screens rob us of this positive emotion by feeding us videos and images of people living in abject poverty. We are conditioned to believe the majority of the world's population is *still* poor. Meanwhile, every day, people in level 1 are moving to level 2, businesses are making in-roads into previously labeled 'developing countries', and level 4 remains oblivious.

Now comes the average age to which most folks live before they die. The average age calculated here, as with all averages, cannot capture all the details, but it is a good indication. At about that time of abject poverty in 1800, life expectancy average was pegged at 30 years all over the world. Today however, that average stands at 72 years. An improvement, right? In fact, another incident that signals marked improvement in this regard is the 1960 famine in China that claimed millions of lives. Doesn't sound much like good news, does it? Well, that famine- which was largely due to poor government administration- was not known to the entire world until a whole 36 years later. China's government did not want to admit that they had failed in this regard so they controlled the news, making sure reports of it did not filter to the outside world.

For one, that would be very impossible in today's interconnected world. Two, no country has to go through that many years of starvation without getting some form of aid from organizations worldwide. You see, even if the world had known about China's famine in 1960, there would still have been little we could do to help. The United Nations food programme didn't take off until 1961.

The averages say Sweden is a Level 4 country. Even though this is an average and doesn't reflect the details of reality, it's a start. We can safely come to the conclusion that the average person in Sweden lives on Level 4. But that was not the case in 1800 and since that time, the country has made remarkable improvements in health and wealth that are worth noting. Also, as at 2017, there were countries living at several levels through which Sweden has passed, from 1800 until now.

- The Sweden into which I was born- in the 1950s- was on a Level 3, same as present-day Egypt.
- 1975 Sweden had improved and was on the verge of Level 4, as 2017 Malaysia is.

It's not always been glamorous however.

- 1921 Sweden was on a Level 2, corresponding with present-day Zambia, and in 1891, it was comparable to what Lesotho is today: between Level 1 and 2.
- Sweden in 1863 was on a strong Level 1 where Afghanistan can be found currently. Most of the population lived in abject poverty and died way early.

But even that has improved. Yes, countries on Level 1 today do not record as many early deaths as Sweden in 1863. So, if you look at it closely, even life on Level 1 has gotten better. Don't assume this progression is peculiar to Sweden. No. Your country has been on the same path. I'm not sure where you reside but I can confidently make this claim because I have facts to prove it. Statistics show that over the last 2 centuries, every country has increased its life expectancy.

Just as with the abject poverty and life expectancy drifts, there are many other things that have gotten better with our world. Unfortunately, our inclination towards the negatives prevent us from accepting facts and encourage despair. Here are some dreadful issues that data shows a decrease in:

- Death penalty
- HIV diseases
- Nuclear arms
- Child mortality
- Legitimate slavery
- Deaths from battles
- Child labor
- Oil spillages
- Leaded gasoline
- Deaths from plane crashes
- Deaths from disaster
- Hunger
- Smallpox
- Ozone depletion
- Pricey solar panels
- Smoke Particles

Facts also show marked improvements in some pretty good stuff you should know:

- Cancer survival rate for children
- Women's right to vote
- Protected nature
- Water
- New movies
- Science
- Harvest
- Girls in school
- Literacy
- Democracy
- Mobile phones
- Monitored species
- Internet
- Wider electricity coverage
- Immunization
- New music

If statistics like these stare us in the face, why are we so fixated on concluding the world is getting worse every day? Yes, you guessed it! Our tendency to spot negatives more than positives. And this is powered by three things:

- **Our inaccurate recollections of past events**

Somehow, human beings have the tendency to view their pasts with rose-colored glasses. You must have heard one or two senior folks lamenting about how things were so much better in their days and how so much has changed these days. They're right about the latter but not so much about the former, because truly so much has changed in the world today, but most of those changes are for the better. This tendency to glamorize the past is not exclusive to older people in Europe or America. For these, we could say maybe most of the present older people did not experience the worst- it was decades ago that their countries were struggling in Level 1. But even in countries like India and China where it wasn't long ago that the majority of their population was in abject poverty, the story is not much different.

One journalist visited India in the 1970s and authored a book detailing the lives of its rural dwellers. When he would visit the same places in the late 1990s, the difference was clear- their houses were more modern, they had access to Television, they wore good clothes, and the people were generally more informed. Interestingly, when this journalist showed them the pictures he had taken on his initial visit, the people found it difficult to believe they had once been that poor. Nobody remembered exactly how it *really* used to be anymore.

- **Biased reporting employed by the press and activists to whip up drama and emotions**

Ever heard the saying, "bad news is good news for the media"? How many times have you turned on the news and saw the report of a plane that took off and landed safely without any hitches? Or a batch of crops that turned out a great harvest as expected? I'm guessing you've not come across such in the news. The media thrives on negative stories- wars, famines, natural disasters, corruption, etc. - that fill us with dread. Increased freedom of the press and advanced technologies also serve as double-edged tools because even though they signify that the world is better than it used to be, they also make it easier than ever before to stuff our heads full with dramatic negative reports dished out by the press. Activists follow a similar path with their dramatic predictions of doom and twisting of statistics to support their causes. Coupled with skewed reporting that instills fear in us, our inclination towards idealizing the past and forgetting that things once used to be worse, promotes a state of perpetual worry.

- **Our hesitance to admit that things are getting better because some things are still bad**

Earlier on, I established that so much of what we know today are feelings and emotions. Folks think they know that the world is deteriorating, but really, it is more about them feeling uncomfortable with the fact that the world is progressing? How can that be when there are still a bunch of world problems we're dealing with, right? It just doesn't sit right with them that I'm bringing up all these facts to the contrary when they can still see problems, so people would rather stick with the easy assumption that the world is getting worse. It wouldn't cost much to wrap their brains around that.

I understand that, as long as there are problems, we must acknowledge them and work continually towards a solution. But I also believe that this should not stop us from acknowledging the progress that has already been made. It's easy to conclude that I have an optimistic worldview, but on a closer look, you'll realize I'm just a man who acknowledges the fact that our world is better than it was many years ago and sees opportunities for it to be even better. The tendency to always see the negative in everything turns us hopeless because we believe that so far nothing has worked; the world keeps deteriorating, so why try anymore? But if we acknowledge the progress our world has made so far, we also embrace the possibilities of making it even better and fuel our motivation to work towards just that.

We need to get to that point where we can beat our innate tendencies to always notice the negative even when everything and everyone around us is walking the opposite path.

First off, the answer does not lie in you stuffing your head with the exclusively positive news. That would be like abandoning one extreme for another. The reality is bad things still happen *and* the world is better today than it was yesterday. Until we can accept both facts, and accept that they are both true at the same time, we cannot overcome the negativity instinct.

Another thing I have found that helps is to always brace yourself for distressing news. The plethora of bad news coming your way daily from the media and advocates of specific causes will affect you less when you keep in mind the fact that their reporting is usually lopsided.

We also need to stop editing our pasts. It may have been unpleasant, but knowing that we're in a better place today can fill us with hope and the strength to tackle existing problems, thereby creating an even better world.

Sweden was in Level 3 when I was born, and during my lifetime, we have moved to Level 4. There has been evident progress, one of which is reduced deaths of children by drowning, and believe it or not, there are many countries today progressing at a faster rate.

CHAPTER THREE: THE STRAIGHT-LINE INSTINCT

Key Takeaways:

- *The third big fallacy is that world population is escalating and must be stopped*
- *We tend to assume the worst when we see statistics on issues we're not conversant with*
- *We have a better balance with nature than they did in the past.*
- *We must learn to think of curves and understand that our world can hardly be represented by a straight line.*

It's interesting that a bunch of numbers possess the ability to instill fear in human beings, but then again, it's not about the numbers. It's what they signify that has the power to evoke strong emotions in us. When, in September of 2014, I saw a WHO graph on the Ebola outbreak in West Africa, it was not the numbers that got me scared. The numbers implied a doubling pattern in the infection rate of Ebola and that, to put it mildly, was terrible news. This was an impending disaster of epic proportions that would sooner spread across the world. Ebola was not like malaria. It was not restricted to particular weather conditions and it could travel across regions. Worse, it had no known cure.

I rallied my team and we started to take action; releasing videos with the purpose of communicating the exigency surrounding the situation. Unfortunately, I could have done so much more way sooner, but like most folks, I had wrongly imagined the increase rate of Ebola cases to be a straight line. In actual fact, the accompanying data showed a replication pattern and I was very late in noticing it.

There's a global rave about world sustainability right now; discussions on optimum human population and what have you. You would expect that folks participating in the discussion would be well informed about trends and patterns in human population growth. Sadly, that is not the case.

The third big fallacy is that the population of the world is escalating, and that it will continue to go on that path if measures are not taken to stop it. It's a one-way pattern of thinking when we see straight lines in everything. What is even more unfortunate is that those who should be authorities on this issue don't seem to know any better. We once asked a group of world population patterns teachers about the United Nations' projection on the number of children by the year 2100. Only a small percentage of them got it right and I couldn't help wondering what they were passing on to their young students.

This predicament was not just about teachers getting a question wrong. It was more. Forecasts on world population trends are usually informed by projected figures of the number of children. So, if we were getting this wrong, we would be getting so many other things wrong as well. As it turned out, the correct answer for the question was the same as the current figures. In other words, there are 2 billion children in the world today and the UN projects that there would still be 2 billion children by the year 2100. No straight, continuous lines here as we are often inclined to believe.

So far, obvious trends of human population growth can be scary. It took about 10,000 years for humans to reach the 1 billion mark. That was in 1800. But since then, the world population has increased by 1 billion in just 130 years, and by a whopping 5 billion in less than a century. Studying this, it is very hard not to conclude that the population just keeps swelling and that if something is not done, there would soon be too many humans struggling for rationed resources. Unfortunately, this can be very misleading in contemporary times.

I have discovered that when people view statistical charts on issues they're not conversant with- like population projections- they tend to assume that the straight line stretches on and on. On the other hand, most people looking at a child's height chart can tell that the line does not just stretch out infinitely. A child does not just continue to grow taller and taller until his parents have to do something drastic to curb the growth. It gets to a stage where it stops and a person stops growing tall. That's exactly how it is with the human population. Experts on the topic project that even though the growth rate has been astronomical for a while now, a slowing trend is being recorded presently. The current population is 7.6billion and experts are predicting that by the end of the century, there'll only be at most, about 12billion.

One of the UN's predictions is that there will be a 4billion-increase in population by the year 2100. Why? Because there'll be more adults than children or the elderly. There won't be more children, or rather there aren't more children already because the world has improved generally. More people are getting out of abject poverty and getting educated; realizing that, to give their children quality lives, they would need to have only a few. The popularity of contraceptives further makes it easier for couples to have less children without having to give up the satisfaction of sex. Back in 1948, the average figure for number of babies per woman was five, and now the figure is less than 2.5.

A population curve remains flat when the number of parents in one generation is replicated in the next. This means the population figures remain mostly the same. This was the case all those tens of thousands of years before 1800. There was no increase but it was for no good reason. During those years, women typically had many children, but because most of those children often died young, they had no chances of growing up and becoming parents themselves. So the population curve did not experience any turbulence. Something similar is happening in our modern-day world, but even better. Instead of a balance occasioned by the sad deaths of young children, we are attaining a balance because we're having lesser children than they did. Between 1999 and the new millennium, there was a multiplied growth. Why? Because parents were having more than two children on the average, and because the world was better than it used to be, those children lived long enough to have their own children. Such is not the case presently. As I mentioned earlier, people are having fewer kids now and a new equilibrium is already a reality.

Not unexpectedly, there are always people on hand to dispute the facts I show and explain. In this case, many still come to me, certain in their perceived knowledge about African societies where people still have many children and where religion plays a major role. Sadly, these people were all victims of the media's skewed reporting that was built for drama. I would later topple the fallacy that religion played a major role in creating large families but I made sure to point out that it is abject poverty that has a statistically proven link to large family creation.

This tendency to imagine that world population will keep growing- as that straight line- infinitely fuels the obsession to 'do something' about it. You'll be surprised the number of learned people who reach out to Melinda Gates asking her to stop spending money taking care of children born into abject poverty. They do not want the world to be overpopulated and they appear to be doing something about it. Their thinking is that the more you save a child from poverty, the greater the chances of population explosion.

Interestingly, that is not how it works. When these children are taken out of poverty and given the opportunity to leave Level 1, they become more informed with the education they can now access. They do not need as many children for chores anymore, and they're not scared that some children may die. Thus, they are enlightened to have fewer children. As it turns out, curbing poverty and providing better quality lives are the major ways to stem the tide. What's more? When parents have fewer children, less children get to die, eventually reducing child mortality rates.

The best way to combat this instinct to see straight lines in everything is to continually remind yourself that curves come in variants, and that, at the end of the day, most of our issues cannot be adequately represented by a straight line.

CHAPTER FOUR: THE FEAR INSTINCT

Key Takeaways:

- *The fear instinct can be traced to our evolutionary ancestors*
- *Fear can serve as a push to achieve great things. It can also pull you into despair.*
- *The media constantly capitalize on our fear instinct.*
- *Your fear of terrorism may just be unnecessary*
- *Scary does not mean dangerous*

In October of 1975, I was a junior doctor in Sweden. On one of those days when it happened that I was the only doctor on the floor, an emergency helicopter landed with victims of a plane crash and what I experienced next was nothing short of a lesson.

The first man I attended to as they rushed in was losing blood- fast- and having a seizure at the same time. But while I was engrossed in taking off his clothing so I could administer the right treatment, he was more interested in saying a bunch of unintelligible stuff. It did not seem like he understood English; his mumbled sounds sounded to me like the Russian language.

Luckily, I knew some Russian, so I told him he was in a hospital in Sweden while moving to shred his military uniform so I could treat. That was it. The terror that clouded his face was like nothing I had ever seen all my life.

Then it hit me out of nowhere! I still cannot explain how my mind arrived at the conclusion but suddenly I was sure World War III was upon us. Of course, the man was bleeding, he was wearing a Military uniform, and had been piloting a Russian war plane when he was shot down in Swedish territory. I froze in fear. As it turned out, the man was a Swedish Air Force pilot whose plane had crashed in icy water during a routine flight. What I thought was seizure was merely shivering from his extended stay in the water, and what I saw as blood was ink spilling from his life jacket that lay on the floor at my feet. I could not have been farther from the truth with my assumptions, and I knew their source.

For so long, I had dreaded my first emergency experience. I was a junior doctor, just starting out and needing all the reassurance I could get. So when I was eventually faced with an emergency experience, I freaked out. My fears of a third world war also came into play. On many nights as a child, I would run to my parents after having a nightmare. I thought that phase was behind me but obviously, it had always been lurking, and when it found the slightest hint of confirmation, it was resuscitated. What is most significant about this experience is that it left me speechless and incapable of any rational thinking. My entire being was numbed by fear, and instead of seeing things as they really were, I saw what I wanted to see.

It's just not humanly possible for us to assimilate every piece of information. It then boils down to what we choose to digest and what we choose to ignore. So far we have learnt that we have the tendency to tilt towards the gap, negative, and dramatic stories, an inclination that the media continue to exploit. They feed us with dramatic stories of the uncommon and the abnormal, and soon enough we're all thinking that's our normal. News of wars, disasters, famine, etc. have left us with a skewed worldview even though we have data to the contrary at our disposal.

Certain fears appear to be consistent among humans, and it's no surprise that these are the same fears exhibited by our evolutionary forefathers for the sake of preservation. They feared

- Injuries to their body
- Confinement of their freedom
- Contamination by poisonous substances.

Take a good look at these basic fears. They are what our news are filled with today, aren't they? And because it is a primal instinct within us, these hazards will always bring out the fear in us. For people living on Level 1 and Level 2, these fears are somewhat practical, but for people on Level 3 and Level 4, they serve no real purpose. Instead, they strengthen phobias and the twisted fear-driven worldview which the media love to capitalize on. Ironically, while the media have become more notorious in their reporting of a world filled with dangers and evils, our world has actually never been more secure. Instinctive fears that were essential to our forebears' survival now assist the media in exploiting our attention pattern.

We asked respondents about how the number of natural disaster deaths has fared in the last hundred years and again, majority got it wrong, going for the option that paints a grim picture. The facts remain that fewer people die today from natural disasters because only a small portion remains in Level 1. Disasters hit Level 1 countries worst because there is no capital to put preventive measures in place, but even at that, the number of natural disaster deaths experienced by Level 1 countries today is lower than ever. There are also technological advancements that make it easier for the rest of the world to rally around affected countries and save more lives.

But most people are not aware of this progress. I know it's hard to think about progress while the News shows images of malnourished children in war-torn countries. It is wrong, to say the least, in all ramifications. Not until the storm has blown past can we pick up on using the facts we have to evaluate our present situation and mapping the agenda for a better future.

Still exploiting our fear instinct, the media conveniently leaves out the impressive number of flights that made safe landings while pushing in our faces, hyped figures of the small percentage that did not make it.

They conveniently leave out the fact that we are living in the most peaceful time throughout history. I'm not saying there are still no wars or conflicts in certain countries. I'm saying that compared to the past, these countries are a small fraction of the world population. I am saying that even though there are still bad happenings, things are getting better.

The case is not much different when it comes to pollution. Altogether, today, there are 15,000 nuclear warheads in the world as against the 64,000 that was available in 1986. Just as our fear instinct pushes us to come together in pursuit of a solution, it can also push us right into the arms of danger. When a tsunami knocked down the nuclear power plant in Fukushima, Japan, it wasn't radioactivity that killed 1,600 people. It was fear.

Unlike every trend we have evaluated, terrorism is on the rise. And next to terrorists, journalists don't even come close in the exploitation of fear. Terrorist activities prey on every one of the fears identified earlier and statistics show that terrorist activities from 2007-2016 have tripled what they were in the previous 10-year window. This is definitely something to be looked into, but facts reveal that terrorist events in Level 4 countries continue to decline and in places like the United States, alcohol-related deaths account for an average of 69,000 persons annually, while terrorism accounts for 159. Yet, the media in these countries always add the dramatic twist to their reportage of terrorist incidents, spiking the people's fears and promoting an inaccurate worldview. A survey was done one week after 9/11 and it revealed that 51% of Americans were scared their family members would fall victim to terrorists. Fourteen years later, the figure is still the same. Fear.

To conquer this instinct, we must be able to differentiate between what is scary and what is truly dangerous. Only then can we stop giving in to fear and living with the wrong mindset.

CHAPTER FIVE: THE SIZE INSTINCT

Key Takeaways:

- *We have a tendency to get carried away by individual figures*
- *The media capitalizes on this tendency to mislead us with big figures with dramatic implications.*
- *To rise above this tendency, we must learn not to consider numbers in isolation*

Many years ago, as a young doctor in Mozambique, I had a very unpleasant task. I was the only doctor in a region that could have done better with at least a hundred. On an average, one child died in our hospital every week, but what was worse was that I bore the responsibility of calculating these deaths and discovered that more children were dying outside the hospital than inside. To save more lives, I had to ration scarce resources. This meant I was not able to give optimum healthcare to the children who came into the hospital. I channeled some of those resources into training the community on hygiene practices that could help reduce the number of children suffering from diarrhea and the like.

Needless to say, I got a lot of backlash from various quarters, including my colleagues who thought it was heartless of me to think about other suffering children instead of thinking solely about my patients. This is the dilemma with Level 1 countries where abject poverty is the norm. It is instinctive to want to do the best possible for the person you can see in obvious pain. It is instinctive to not care at that moment for the bigger picture filled with many more sufferers. But these only lead to more deaths and more suffering.

The propensity to misinterpret things is very common among us humans, and just as with our inclinations to notice negatives or give in to our fears, the media capitalizes on our tendency to get carried away by size and reach misguided conclusions. The press preys on the fact that we are easily moved by the sight of a person suffering, so they take one story of one individual and attach to it, way more significance than they should. Thus, we believe the world is getting worse. We do not see the improvements in our world because we do not come across reports of them in the news, but we see the person suffering and automatically assume the whole world is suffering.

During my time in Mozambique, there were many who thought I was a villain for not being consumed with the patients I could see. Yet, statistics prove that child survival rates are not higher now because of treatments but as a result of an increase in preventive methods and mostly, increased literacy among mothers. This realization is highly significant in providing health aids for Level 1 and Level 2 countries. The focus should not be on the provision of hospitals and expensive treatment procedures, but on preventive education for medical staff and the people.

To squelch this tendency, you must:

- **Never consider a number in isolation because that is never the case**

Numbers represent people, issues, occurrences, etc., and these are never isolated. They exist and occur in interaction with a million and one other things. Looking at a number and running assumptions with it can be very misleading so learn to always evaluate one figure- especially big ones- in relation to another. Take for instance, the reported UNICEF figures of the number of baby deaths in 2016: a whopping 4.2million! 4.2million babies who all died before they reached the age of one! Very shocking indeed! But when you compare it to the 4.4million figure for 2015, and the 4.5million for 2014, or even the 14.4million figure for 1950, you're able to see a more accurate picture. Suddenly, 4.2million does not sound so big anymore. In fact, it becomes small. We can accurately tell that although 4.2million babies dying is bad, the situation is getting better.

- **Always divide a figure by the larger sum**

Until you ascertain the significance of a particular figure, it is easy to run out of proportion and make inaccurate conclusions. The media, charity organizations, and activist are very good at bombarding us with big figures that carry dramatic implications, but when those figures are divided by the total population, the meaning completely changes and it is only then that we can ascertain their real significance. Consider again the 4.2million baby deaths in 2016. With the help of simple division, we can ascertain the implication of this figure. In 1950 when there were 97million births and the death rate was 14.4million, the child mortality rate stood at 15 percent. In 2016 however, there were 141million births, and when you divide that figure by 4.2million, you have a 3 percent rate of child mortality! The figures make more sense now, don't they?

CHAPTER SIX: THE GENERALIZATION INSTINCT

Key Takeaways:

- *Classifications make our world more orderly but they can also twist our perceptions.*
- *No two persons or countries should be assumed as the same*
- *The media may not be the best place to consult for a real representation of the world.*
- *Experiencing other levels first-hand is one of the ways to avoid falling prey*

Once when I was doing some research work on one of the remotest regions in the world, myself and my colleague were treated to an appreciation party by the inhabitants who lived in abject poverty. The first course was a grilled rat and even though I was nauseated to say the least, I ate it out of consideration for our hosts. When it was time to eat their dessert of larvas however, I just could not go further. It was quite a scene though as my Danish colleague was already sucking away at the squishy things. I was left looking like the impolite one so I figured my best bet was to lie. I told them the

Swedish culture forbade eating of larvas and that my colleague could eat it only because it was okay to do so in Denmark. Upon hearing this, they backed off. It was a shared understanding that people from different places had different practices and traditions.

The truth is, as much as we speak against generalizations, it is something humans find natural and easy to do. To some extent, putting things or people into boxes help us to create order in our world. Yet, this same tendency, taken too far, pushes us to draw inaccurate conclusions about various aspects of our world. We hastily fill our preconceived boxes with people and countries and assume everyone or every country in one box are all the same. Based on our inaccurate perceptions of the world, we think inaccurately and act inaccurately. Worse still, the media cashes in on this again, constantly creating and reinforcing stereotypes that feed our predisposition to lump things together. Our tendency to create divisions lead us to imagine the world as an 'US versus THEM' arena, and with the tendency to generalize, we hastily conclude that the 'THEM' are all the same. This misconception plays out in our actions and decisions. For instance, multinational corporations that refuse to explore business opportunities in certain countries because they fall into a specific 'category'.

Take producers of sanitary pads for example, they continue to miss the mark because they are so fixated on a worldview fueled by incorrect generalizations. Instead of penetrating Level 2 and 3 markets, their major focus is on creating more innovative products for an already-saturated Level 4 market.

Statistics show that the number of babies per woman is reducing globally, which means less pregnancies.

Good news for pad manufacturers.

More women are educated globally, which means more users of hygiene menstruation methods.

Again, good news for pad manufacturers.

More women are working in offices globally, which means they'll definitely need something to stay clean while at work.

Good news again!

But have all these facts influenced decisions of top pad manufacturers (who happen to be mostly Western)? Not so much, because they're stuck with a mental imagery of the world's majority. And thanks to the media's reinforcement of stereotypes, those images are not usually pretty.

One of the major reasons why it's so easy to generalize is that we don't know everything or everybody. Our knowledge is limited so we instinctively make up for it by summing up everything else in the little we know. It's also the reason why the media is largely successful in its reinforcement of stereotypes. It acts as a leans through which we view the world but unfortunately, it focuses on the unusual; the peculiar cases that do not reflect reality. To rid ourselves of this tendency, we need to become more aware, not by trusting the media but by experiencing things and people for ourselves. We need to travel and see how people live in their countries. You'll be surprised at some of the insights you'll gather!

Alternative ways of avoiding this trap exist:

- Consult the Dollar Street project, a collection of real-life photographs of families living on different levels across the world. You'll realize how different these images are from google or the media.

- Constantly evaluate your classifications. Examine aspects of life where people within the same class differ and cases where people in different classes have a likeness. Understand that a majority fact is not enough to label the entire group. Be careful of unusual samples singled out to draw conclusions on the whole.
- Stop concluding that your way of life is the norm. This closes your mind to the validity of other people's experiences and can leave you feeling like anyone living differently from you is wrong.
- Avoid lumping different groups in one generalization. Whether you see it or not, each group has its peculiarities even if it bears similarities to another.

CHAPTER SEVEN: THE DESTINY INSTINCT

Key Takeaways:

- *Our tendency to believe some people or countries can never change promotes a lopsided worldview*
- *Some African countries have progressed at a rate higher than that of some European countries.*
- *Progression, regardless of how small or how slow, is significant.*
- *Knowledge about humans can never be static because humans are never static. Keep an open mind.*

I recently made a presentation on the economic viability of Asia and Africa to a couple of Capital administrators and their richest clients. The purpose of that presentation was to get the wealthy clients to see why they needed to stop pumping money into saturated markets in European countries and start looking towards potential markets in Asia and Africa. After the presentation in which I managed to surprise most of my audience with the facts, an old man walked up to me. He started off by saying how impressive my presentation was, then he gave me his opinion, or as one might call it, worldview: that there was just no way Africa could have such potential as I had presented because it was just in them not to do so. That old man, though he may not have known it, was expressing his tendency to believe that certain things were not possible because they are fated or destined not to be.

Unfortunately, there are many people who have this instinct. We believe that some people or countries are just made in some kind of way, or that they have certain intrinsic characteristics that make them who they are, and that no matter what happens, they can never change. Many years ago when our evolutionary ancestors lived in communities that remained the same for a long time, this instinct might have served them well, but in today's world, it only impedes our ability to recognize the phenomenal improvements taking place globally. It closes our minds and perpetuates the superiority of certain groups and inferiority of others. Let's not forget also that this kind of twisted worldview continues to cost us potential business goldmines.

Contrary to this worldview, people change, cultures change, countries change. And they change all the time. Here also, the media is an obvious culprit with its stereotypical reporting that portrays our world as unchanging.

Statistics do not support the instinct that Africa is fated to be poor and subordinate to the West. True, there are still bad things and when you look at the improvement numbers in isolation, you might be tempted to believe the destiny instinct. But when you consider those numbers in comparison with what obtained many years back, you'll come to realize that some African countries have indeed experienced improvements at a faster rate than some European countries. Sadly, many investors and business owners are blinded by the fallacy that Africa is fated to be poor and are missing out on the potential of its large middle-income market.

Muslims are not fated to have more babies as is the popular perception. Instead, statistics show that it is people living on Level 1, regardless of their religious affiliation, who have more babies. Similarly, certain attributes like openness with sex issues are instinctively attributed to certain countries- like Sweden- as though it had always been. But that is not the case. Growing up, I still remember a time when parents did not talk about sex with their children and when abortion was illegal and morally frowned upon.

But today, young people find it difficult to imagine such times ever existed in Sweden because the society is now far from what it used to be.

There are a couple of measures that can be taken to check this tendency:

- Avoid writing off small and slow improvements. Little drops of water make a mighty ocean, and small improvements still count as improvements. The Level 4's of today did not attain their status in a day.
- Keep an open mind when it comes to knowledge and facts about the world you live in. People change. Cultures change. Countries change.
- Make a comparison between your current standards and what existed in the times of your parents and grandparents. It's most likely that you'll be faced with evidence of change from one generation to another.
- Remind yourself constantly of how cultures have changed in different countries over the years.

CHAPTER EIGHT: THE SINGLE PERSPECTIVE INSTINCT

Key Takeaways:

- *Holding on to a single school of thought makes it easier to assess the world, but it also promotes an inaccurate view of the world.*
- *Experts, activists, and political enthusiasts are notorious for single perspectives*
- *No one idea or approach can solve all of life's problems*

By now we all know how dangerous it is to form perceptions of the world based on what the media portrays, but if we can't trust the media to give us accurate information about our world, who then do we trust? Professionals? Even here, we must exercise caution.

The single perspective instinct is expressed in our tendency to run off feeling we have something figured out because we happen to come across some insight.

We hold on stubbornly to that one idea that we came by and refuse to certain anything to the contrary. Inevitably, every world problem is interpreted in line with this one-sided perspective and every solution is proffered based on the same. A one-dimensional mindset is an easy way out. Instead of assessing every issue distinctively, we just dissect it in line with pre-conceived ideas. Unfortunately, this gives us an inaccurate perspective of our world and makes us resistant to change. Nothing about human beings and society is certain. You must keep an open mind and not be overly critical of ideas that seem to contradict yours. You have to be willing to see the world through the lenses of other people. Motives behind a one-dimensional inclination are either tied to professional emphasis or political leanings.

Professionals contribute immensely to the progress of our world. They provide us with reliable data with which we can clearly understand the world. Ironically however, their strength is also their weakness. Professionals are regarded as such because they are specialists in their respective fields; authorities who have dedicated the most part of their lives to studying a particular aspect of life. This very fact strengthens in them a single perspective instinct. They are so immersed in their respective fields that everything and everyone else in the world is viewed through their fixated lenses. By the very nature of their career, they possess advanced knowledge. The problem is, that knowledge often explains only a small fraction of the world's reality. This tendency is usually more pronounced in activists and advocates who, most of the time, are blinded to facts by their passion for a cause. In the bid to whip up support for their causes, they ignore the improvements that have been made in that regard and promote the perspective of a world that is getting worse.

The simplistic perspective instinct promotes a couple of things that we should look out for:

- Figures are useful but it is what lies beneath them- what they imply- that carries significance. Figures alone cannot solve world problems.
- Contrary to what many medical practitioners believe, medicine alone cannot solve the world's problems. This has been demonstrated in many instances where medicine failed because there was a lack of more basic pre-requisites which medicine cannot provide

The single perspective inclination fueled by political leanings are even worse and usually carry weightier consequences. Once after delivering a presentation about the health situation in Cuba, the Minister of Health was proud to announce that their country was the healthiest among poor nations. He was not concerned about their poor status, making it seem like it was normal. Thanks to his one-track mind, he could not see that they could as well be the poorest of the healthy.

No one idea or approach can solve all of life's problems. This is just a fallacy propagated by the single perspective instinct.

CHAPTER NINE: THE BLAME INSTINCT

Key Takeaways:

- *Blaming an individual is a simplistic approach to issues*
- *When things go wrong or right, look to the systems involved, not an individual*

During one of my lectures with a group of students, I mentioned how top pharmaceutical companies were not spending money on research for those illnesses that mostly affected the poor. Quickly, the class turned into a back-and-forth exchange on who should be punched in the face for that situation.

It's human. We all tend to look for someone or something to hold responsible for unpleasant things. It's like a reflex: we hear of something bad and immediately we're thinking of who or what should take the fall for it. This tendency makes it difficult for us to be realistic in our assessment of the world. Once we place the blame at someone's feet, we lose the urge to examine the situation factually. It is this instinct that causes us to overstate the significance or role of certain persons or groups. The same applies to remarkable events. We're quick to attribute such to a certain individual or group, and often times, it's just not that simple.

We have been playing at this blame sport for so long that there are specific groups that constantly show up on our blame radar. This is mostly due to the fact that we are inclined to blaming people that confirm our existing stereotypes. These groups include:

- **Businesses**. It's quite easy to put blame on businesses and corporations, especially the big ones. Prevailing perception is that they are sinister individuals out to make a profit at all cost, even if that means hurting people.

- **The Media.** News agencies and journalists are constantly accused of propagating fake news but at the end of the day, journalists are human like me and you. They also fall victim to the same fallacies we do. How can we expect them to provide an accurate picture of our world when they don't know any better?

- **Foreigners**. Thanks to our 'US versus THEM' complex, we are usually quick to point fingers at others when bad things happen. It would interest you to know that many people in the

West blame development in Asia and Africa for climate change, conveniently ignoring the fact that the bulk of activities that trigger climate change come from the West.

In the same way we overemphasize the role of certain people in unpleasant events, we also overestimate the role of certain others in the realization of landmark improvements. Take for instance the drop in birth rates in China. For most folks, this development was as a result of Mao's one-child policy. But facts reveal that this was not the case. The reduction in birth rates had occurred way before Mao's policy so there is no way Mao gets credit for the improvement. As has been mentioned frequently, this change is attributed to the increase in women literacy and a reduction of people living in abject poverty.

In line with the suggestion that systems, and not individuals, should be evaluated when unpleasant things happen, there is also the need to look at systems when positive developments are made. Most of the time, we're praising the wrong people and ignoring the systems that orchestrated the process. For one, institutions do not get the praise they deserve. Meanwhile, these are the machinery that set in motion various processes of development. The men and women who work behind the scenes in these institutions are the real heroes. Technology is another largely unrecognized hero of our time. To think of all the time saved getting chores done, and the ease with which we access millions of resources on the Internet! Technology truly deserves a 'Thank You'.

We need to avoid pointing fingers at any bad guy because things are not always that simple. Usually, when things go wrong or right, it is as a result of interactions between many entities, and until we can understand that, our view of the world will remain inaccurate.

CHAPTER TEN: THE URGENCY INSTINCT

Key Takeaways:

- *Doing something immediately can mean doing something wrong*
- *The urgency instinct makes rational thinking impossible*
- *This instinct can also lead to a desensitization towards every problem, even genuine ones*
- *Avoid exaggerated claims of world danger. Always consult the data at hand*
- *The solution is not to worry about everything or worry about nothing. It is to worry only about what is important.*

They say "patience is a virtue", but sadly it doesn't appear to be instinctive. Back in 1981 when I was in Mozambique, a certain strange illness was spreading among the people and for a while, I was clueless about what it was. It was of no small significance that I, the only doctor attending to my district, was unable to diagnose what was attacking the people. In panic, and because I was not sure of the nature of this disease, I asked my wife and kids to leave for the city. This move did not go unnoticed by the district mayor, a man known for his ability to take swift action. He posted a question to me that, till this day, I wish I could go back and answer differently. He asked me if I thought he should set up a roadblock and prevent movement into and out of the district and I answered Yes. I told him he had to act. That decision cost us the lives of over 20 women and children. All because someone had to do something!

We go through life submitting to the pressure to do. Just do something NOW, even if it ends up being the wrong thing! Sales representatives have mastered the art of promoting this 'Act Now' message and so have activists who go to extremes just to whip up support for their causes. They are aware that as humans, we have a tendency to want to do something, take a step, make the decision, pick a side, or do whatever else it is that makes us feel we're being 'productive', and they're weighing in on that.

This instinct was more imperative for our evolutionary ancestors as it must have meant the difference between life and death. Humans living with the thought of crossing paths with a lion anytime had little need for complex thought processes. They *had to* act immediately. But the many dangers that our forefathers faced are no longer existent in our world. Our problems today are more complex and require critical thinking. Sure, this instinct still serves us in exceptional emergency situations, but when we let it take over every aspect of our lives, it robs us of the ability to remain logical or think things through analytically.

Interestingly, this tendency does not seem so strong when we're dealing with potential dangers that are far off in the future. This is why activists go all out to convince us of the urgency of their cause. They make us think we have to do something about it now for the sake of posterity. While trying to get us to take action, they increase our stress levels and distort our worldview by making us think all is not well. And more often than not, this instinct leads to terrible decisions with terrible consequences.

On the split side, an over-activation of this tendency makes it lose effectiveness. When someone continues to make outrageous claims designed to scare us, we eventually get used to it and it loses any form of significance.

Climate change experts and activists have often relied on the urgency instinct to provoke a change in people. However, bombarding people with twisted facts designed to scare them into action may produce initial results, but in the long run, people will discover your exaggeration and hyped claims, and then you'll lose their trust and their attention. Trust me, winning those back is always difficult, if not impossible.

In cases of impending danger, the temptation is high to exaggerate reality to initiate a course of action in people. At that point, it almost seems irrelevant to obsess over some data when you could be telling people how at risk the world was and how they had to act immediately. But this is not the way to go. Often times, when we ignore data and go the dramatic route, we end up losing our way.

In 2014 when Liberia was facing the Ebola crisis, a lot was being done. Test samples were being collected, suspected cases were being quarantined, people were being urged to reduce all forms of contact and maintain optimum hygiene. Yet, no one was taking the time to collate and analyze the data. When I stepped in and had my son make sense of the existing figures, it turned out the number of cases had been decreasing without anyone noticing. The people lived their lives in constant worry and pressure, not having any idea that they were gradually winning the war against Ebola. When the health workers got the interpretation of this data, it filled them with hope and spurred them to do more.

Exploiting the urgency instinct has robbed many of their capacity to care about anything anymore. Incessant scare tactics have numbed us to any raised world concern. This is sad because there are real issues that have global effects and future implications. These issues genuinely deserve our concern because they could hinder global human development for years and no, these are not perceived risks. They are dangers that the world has experienced before.

- Epidemics of global proportions
- Financial catastrophe
- The possibility of another world war
- Climate change
- Abject poverty

The two extremes to the urgency instinct are worrying about everything and worrying about nothing. The solution therefore is to be concerned only about the important stuff, like the five issues listed above. We must quench the urge to act immediately and instead engage in critical with the help of existing relevant data.

CHAPTER ELEVEN: FACTFULNESS IN PRACTICE

Key Takeaways:

- *Factfulness is relevant in every aspect of our human life.*
- *A worldview based on concrete facts is a possibility... And a process.*

Practicing factfulness has nothing to do with literacy or whether a person lives in Level 1 or Level 4. In 1989, it was an uneducated, barefoot woman who saved me from being butchered by an angry mob in one of the farthest parts of Africa. I had gone on a research assignment to study the same disease I had earlier encountered in Mozambique. My big mistake was not speaking with the people I had come to help. I did not tell them why I would be visiting their houses, why I would be asking them questions, or why I would be taking their blood samples. It was obvious this mob was scared. Their fear instincts had been set off by my intention to take their blood samples and because they had classified me as a typical pillaging white man, they were sure I was going to sell their blood. Now, they were ready to act immediately to combat what they perceived as an immediate threat.

But, after I explained my mission through an interpreter, it was this woman, one of the mobs, who came out and pleaded my case to her people. She delivered a rational presentation of my mission, highlighting the effects of the disease and the need to let me help them find a solution. She factually recalled the time when measles was killing their young and how a team of white people had returned with a vaccine after collecting their blood. It was she who saved my life.

Factfulness should be ingrained in every aspect of our day-to-day living;

- In our education system where children need to be taught from a fact-based perspective, making them true global citizens.
- In our businesses where we need to stop making decisions based on stereotypical assumptions.
- As members of the press, activists, and politicians, because we have a duty to report and present an accurate picture of the world.

As difficult as it may appear to one day have a world where everyone sees the world through the clear lens of facts, it is necessary and possible. It may not happen in one day, just as most other changes happen in small increments, but it can be a reality. Then, we can stop living stressful, misguided lives because we think the world is getting worse, and we can channel our energies to making it an even better place.